THE SHOSHONE

A TRUE BOOK®

by

Christin Ditchfield

Children's Press®
A Division of Scholastic Inc.

New York Toronto London Auckland Sydney
Mexico City New Delhi Hong Kong
Danbury, Connecticut

Reading Consultant
Jeanne Clidas, Ph.D.
*National Reading Consultant
and Professor of Reading,
SUNY Brockport*

Content Consultant
Randy'L He-dow Teton, BAFA,
Shoshone-Bannock/Cree

Dedication:
For Ellie Kay, With Love

A dancer at the
Shoshone-Bannock Festival

Library of Congress Cataloging-in-Publication Data

Ditchfield, Christin.
    The Shoshone / by Christin Ditchfield.— 1st American ed.
        p. cm. — (A true book)
Includes bibliographical references and index.
Contents: People of the Great Basin—Living on the land—The Shoshone
family—Celebrating life—The end of the old way—The Shoshone today.
    ISBN 0-516-22987-7 (lib. bdg.)   0-516-24643-7 (pbk.)
    1. Shoshoni Indians—Juvenile literature. [1. Shoshoni Indians.]
I. Title. II. Series.
E99.S4D57 2003
978.004'9745—dc21   2003004544

CHILDREN'S PRESS, and A TRUE BOOK®, and associated logos are
trademarks and or registered trademarks of Scholastic Library Publishing.
SCHOLASTIC and associated logos are trademarks and or registered
trademarks of Scholastic Inc.

1 2 3 4 5 6 7 8 9 10 R 12 11 10 09 08 07 06 05 04 03

Contents

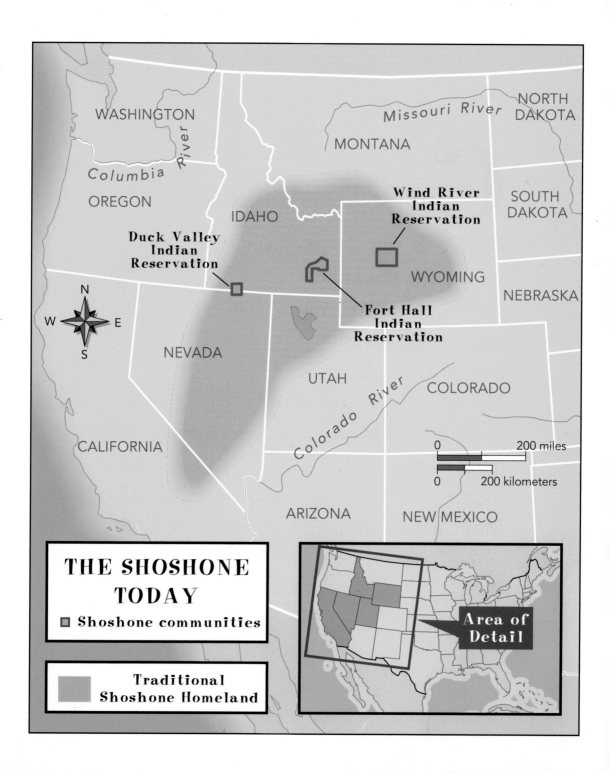

WASHINGTON

Columbia River

OREGON

IDAHO

MONTANA

Missouri River

NORTH DAKOTA

SOUTH DAKOTA

Wind River Indian Reservation

WYOMING

NEBRASKA

Duck Valley Indian Reservation

Fort Hall Indian Reservation

N
W E
S

NEVADA

UTAH

Colorado River

COLORADO

CALIFORNIA

ARIZONA

NEW MEXICO

0   200 miles

0   200 kilometers

THE SHOSHONE TODAY

◻ Shoshone communities

Area of Detail

Traditional Shoshone Homeland

People of the Great Basin

For more than a thousand years, the Shoshone (sho-SHONE) people have lived in the western part of North America. The region in which they live is called the Great Basin because it forms a giant bowl containing all the valleys between the Sierra Nevada and the Rocky Mountains.

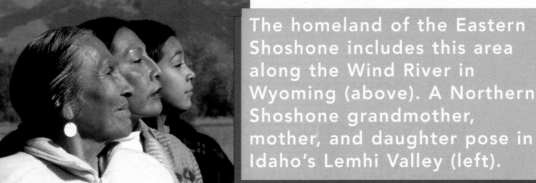

The homeland of the Eastern Shoshone includes this area along the Wind River in Wyoming (above). A Northern Shoshone grandmother, mother, and daughter pose in Idaho's Lemhi Valley (left).

For centuries, the Shoshone traveled from place to place throughout the Great Basin. They lived in valleys and mountains, hills and plains. Eventually, they divided into three large groups.

The Western Shoshone lived in parts of Utah, Nevada, and California. The Northern Shoshone lived in northern Utah, Idaho, and Montana. The Eastern Shoshone lived along the Wind River in southern Wyoming.

The Shoshone did not settle in a particular area. Instead, each group moved from place to place within its own territory. The people were constantly searching for food. Very little rain came across the high mountains. The valleys were often as dry as deserts. Nothing grew in large amounts or for very long. The land could not support large groups of people living in one place. There was simply not enough food or water.

So the Shoshone broke up into smaller bands. A band was made up of several families, perhaps twenty or thirty people in all. Each band learned to make good use of the **resources** in its area. The Shoshone named each band for the foods its people ate most often. For instance, some bands

The Western Shoshone lived in some of the harshest areas of the Great Basin (above). This photo shows a Shoshone encampment in the Wind River Mountains in the late 1800s (right).

were known as "Salmon Eaters." Others were called "Rabbit Eaters" or "Bigsheep Eaters."

Living Off the Land

The Shoshone showed an amazing ability to **adapt** to the harsh conditions of the Great Basin. They learned which types of plants grew in certain areas during different seasons. Shoshone women knew which plants were **edible** or **medicinal**. They gathered

This photograph from the early 1900s shows a Shoshone woman separating grain from the seeds of wild grasses.

Traditional Shoshone foods included chokecherries (a type of wild cherry), dried venison (deer meat), and various kinds of roots and bulbs.

pine nuts, ryegrass seed, roots, and berries. They used some plants and herbs to treat illnesses. They used other plant fibers to weave baskets for storing and carrying food.

The Piñon Tree

Every autumn, the Shoshone headed to areas where piñon trees could be found to gather pine nuts. These sweet, oily pine nuts could be shelled and roasted or eaten raw. The Shoshone often ground the nuts into powder and mixed it with water. The powder became a type of mush, or cereal, that could be eaten hot or cold. A family of four could gather as much as 1,200 pounds (544.8 kilograms) of pine nuts. This supply would last for months, feeding them throughout the long, hard winter.

Piñon trees in Utah (top) and pine nuts (bottom)

Shoshone men hunted for birds, fish, rabbits, deer, and bighorn sheep. Some went further out to the Great Plains to hunt buffalo. One band, called the *Comanches*, or "warriors of the plains," went to hunt buffalo one season and never returned home. Their **descendants** now reside in Oklahoma.

The Shoshone had to be skilled at using a variety of hunting tools and techniques.

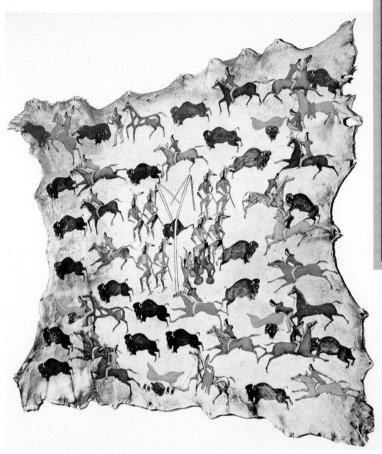

The Western Shoshone lived mainly on seeds, plants, and small animals. The Northern and Eastern Shoshone, who lived closer to the Great Plains, hunted buffalo, as shown in this elk-skin painting.

They captured their **prey** using bows and arrows, knives made of a hard black rock called obsidian, nets, and traps.

All Shoshone spoke the same language, but bands that lived in different areas created their own ways of life. They developed their own beliefs and customs. In cold weather, some lived in caves or shelters dug into hillsides. Some made cone-shaped lodges out of grass, rushes, and willows. In the hot summer months, some built huts out of sticks and branches. Many Shoshone lived in tents called tepees.

Some Shoshone used brush-wood to build temporary shelters called wicki´ups (above). After coming into contact with Plains Indians, many Northern and Eastern Shoshone began living in tepees (right).

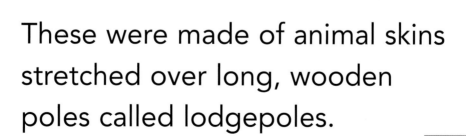

These were made of animal skins stretched over long, wooden poles called lodgepoles.

In the Great Basin, summer temperatures could climb higher than 100° Fahrenheit (38° Celsius). On hot days, the Shoshone wore very little clothing. Men wore loincloths made of deerskin or rabbit skin. Women wore aprons or skirts made of grass. In the winter, temperatures often dropped below 0° Fahrenheit (–18° Celsius). Then the Shoshone wore thicker shirts or wing dresses and leggings

Photos from the 1800s showing a
Shoshone man dressed for warm weather
and a Shoshone woman wearing a dress
decorated with elk teeth

made from animal skins. They
bundled up in warm robes of
deer, elk, or buffalo skins.

19

The Shoshone Family

In a Shoshone family, each member had an important role. Shoshone men hunted wild animals for food. They used the animal skins to make heavy winter clothing. They built the family homes. They protected the family from danger.

Shoshone women gathered plants to use for food or

A Shoshone family in the late 1800s

medicine. They made clothing, jewelry, and many household items. Shoshone women knew how to make pottery, but they were considered expert bas-ketweavers. For people who

Shoshone women have long been known for their beautiful beadwork (top left) and baskets (top right). As this photo (right) from a Shoshone celebration shows, many Shoshone mothers still carry their babies in traditional carriers.

traveled constantly, lightweight, sturdy baskets were much more useful than heavy clay pots. Shoshone women raised the children. They carried their babies on their backs in frames made of willow covered with deerskin.

Shoshone children worked right along with their parents. Boys helped their fathers and girls helped their mothers. Every member of the band did his or her part to hunt and gather food. It was the only way the family could survive.

Most Shoshone bands did not have a chief or an organized system of leadership. Instead, the oldest and wisest members helped the band to make important decisions. Every morning, the Shoshone prayed to "Our Father"—the creator of heaven and Earth. They called him "Appáh." The Shoshone did not have priests or religious leaders. Instead, each person was in tune with the great spirit.

The Shoshone were guided by **visions** and dreams. At various times throughout the year,

Today the Shoshone build their sweatlodges by constructing a willow frame and then covering it with layered blankets.

they held ceremonies inside sweatlodges—dome-shaped huts of sticks covered with animal skins or mud. Today the Shoshone still use sweatlodges daily to ask the spirits for help in healing themselves, family members, and the tribe.

Celebrating Life

Although Shoshone life was hard, it was not all work. Families found time to laugh, play, and sing. In fact, singing was a favorite Shoshone activity. The Shoshone sang constantly throughout the day. They used drums and flutes as instruments.

Drumming is still an important part of Shoshone culture.

As part of their religious ceremonies, the Shoshone often danced together. These dances, which included the Sun Dance and the Ghost Dance, are still

done today. Each dance had its own special steps and movements. Children learned to do the dances at an early age by watching their parents and grandparents.

The Shoshone also enjoyed all kinds of games. Both males and females participated in relay races, chased hoops, threw arrows at targets, ran horse races, and juggled mud

Shoshone men participating in a relay race today

Shoshone women playing the hand game in the 1940s

balls. They even played a kind of football or soccer, called *shinny*, with a ball made of animal skin and stuffed with feathers. The "hand game," however, was the most popular game. Several people secretly passed an object back and forth. Another person tried to guess who was holding the object. This game could go on for hours.

At harvest time each year, Shoshone bands came together from all over the Great Basin. For some friends and family members, it was the first time they had seen each other in months. This was a time of celebration. Everyone shared family news. They introduced new babies who had been born in the last year. They remembered loved ones who had died. Children played games. Single young people looked for someone to marry. This was the way most Shoshone found husbands or wives.

The annual festival often lasted for two or three weeks. Every evening, the people gathered around the fire. They sang and danced and prayed. Sometimes they settled arguments or disputes between various bands. But mostly, they

Today, the Shoshone continue to hold festivals to celebrate and honor their rich heritage.

laughed and shared stories late into the night. Because they had no written language, the young Shoshone learned their family histories by listening to older people tell stories about the past.

Settlers Arrive

For centuries, the Shoshone lived peacefully in the Great Basin. They had little contact with the outside world. Then in 1804, President Thomas Jefferson sent a group of explorers, led by Meriwether Lewis and William Clark, to scout out the land beyond the Mississippi River. He wanted them to see if

Lewis and Clark meeting Shoshone people in 1805

they could find their way to the Pacific Ocean. The explorers discovered all the wonders of the West.

Soon, thousands of white settlers began moving into the

Sacagawea

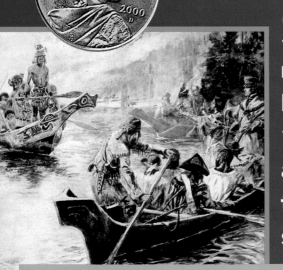

Sacagawea was often able to translate for Lewis and Clark when they met other American Indian peoples during their journey.

Sacagawea is one of the most famous American Indian women in history. In 1804, Sacagawea served as an expert guide and **translator**. With her infant son on her back, she led the explorers Lewis and Clark through the wilderness across North America. This Shoshone woman showed more courage and strength than the forty-three men who traveled with her. More than once, she risked her life to save them. They later admitted that they could not have made it without her.

Today Sacagawea is **immortalized** on the golden U.S. dollar (shown above). The model for the coin is Shoshone-Bannock tribal member Randy'L He-dow (Meadowlark) Teton, of the Northern Shoshone.

Life changed forever for the Shoshone people after white settlers began moving westward in the 1800s.

Great Basin. They built their homes right in the middle of Shoshone territory. Others passed through the area on their way to Oregon and California. The land could not support all these people. The natural environment was destroyed—

and so was the Shoshone way of life. They could no longer find the plants and animals they needed for food.

Some of the Shoshone fought to protect their lands. One of the few Shoshone chiefs, Chief Washakie, saw that it was useless to try to drive the whites out. There were too many of them. He urged his people to make peace with their new neighbors.

Eventually, white settlers took over all of the Shoshone land. They forced the Shoshone people

Chief Washakie of the Eastern Shoshone (center) thought he could best protect his people by maintaining good relations with the U.S. government.

to move to certain areas called **reservations**—and stay there. The Shoshone could no longer live the way they had in the past. They had to find a new way to live.

The Shoshone Today

Today, more than twelve thousand Shoshone live in the United States. Most Shoshone live on reservations in Idaho, Nevada, Wyoming, Utah, and California. In many ways, the Shoshone live just like any other Americans. They wear the same clothes and drive the same cars. They live and work in the city and countryside. They

work as doctors and lawyers and
engineers.

At the same time, they preserve
their history and culture. They
want to pass on the Shoshone
traditions to the next **generation.**
There are newspapers and magazines that celebrate the Shoshone
way of life. Websites and online
groups help members of the

tribe connect with one another. Some people have recorded elderly Shoshone people telling old stories and family histories. Others have created a written form of the Shoshone language so it can be taught to young people.

Every year in August, hundreds of people gather at the Shoshone-Bannock Indian Festival. They sing old and new songs and perform old and new dances. They share traditional arts and crafts and recipes. They play the games that the Shoshone have played for hundreds of years. They also have a

The ground-blessing ceremony for a cultural center in Idaho devoted to Sacagawea (above) and kids on a parade float during the Shoshone-Bannock Festival (right)

rodeo, parades, pageant contests, and a softball tournament. These are some of the many ways the Shoshone people celebrate their past, present, and future.

To Find Out More

Here are some additional resources to help you learn more about the Shoshone:

 **Books**

Gleiter, Jan. **Sacagawea.** Raintree Steck-Vaughn Publishers, 1998.

Mattern, Joanne. **The Shoshone People.** Bridgestone Books, 2001.

Miller, Jay. **American Indian Families.** Children's Press, 1997.

Miller, Jay. **American Indian Festivals.** Children's Press, 1997.

Moss, Nathaniel. **The Shoshone Indians.** Chelsea House Publishers, 1997.

Thomasma, Kenneth. **Naya Nuki: Shoshoni Girl Who Ran.** Grandview Publishing Company, 2003.

Thomasma, Kenneth. **The Truth About Sacajawea.** Grandview Publishing Company, 1998.

⚡ Organizations and Online Sites

Eastern Shoshone Tribe
http://www.Eastern Shoshone.net

This site includes information about the history and culture of the Eastern Shoshone, as well as facts about the Wind River Reservation in Wyoming.

Lewis and Clark: The Journey of the Corps of Discovery
http://www.pbs.org/ lewisandclark

On this site you can browse an archive of the nearly fifty American Indian peoples encountered by Lewis and Clark during their 8,000-mile (12,872-km) journey. This site includes learning activities to help students "relive" the adventure of this historic expedition.

NativeWeb: Resources for Indigenous Cultures Around the World
http://www.nativeweb.org

This site lists more than 4,000 historical and contemporary resources related to 250 separate nations.

Shoshone-Bannock Tribes
http://www. shoshonebannocktribes.com

This site tells about the history of the Shoshone and Bannock Indians, describes the annual Shoshone-Bannock Festival, and includes current news.

Utah History to Go— Shoshoni Indians
http://historytogo.utah. gov/shoshone.html

This site includes a good summary of the history of the Shoshone.

Shoshoni Language Home Page
http://www.isu.edu/ ~loetchri/

This site contains an introduction to the Shoshoni alphabet, an English-Shoshoni dictionary, and easy-to-read stories in Shoshoni.

Important Words

adapt to change to fit a new situation

descendants relatives of people who lived long ago

edible able to be eaten safely

generation people born around a certain time

immortalized made forever famous

medicinal able to be used as medicine

prey animal that is hunted for food

reservations areas of land set aside by the government as places for American Indians to live

resources supplies of things that people use to help them survive

translator person who speaks more than one language and helps others communicate

visions images that appear to someone, as in a dream

Index

Meet the Author

Christin Ditchfield is an author and conference speaker, and is host of the nationally syndicated radio program *Take It To Heart!* Her articles have been featured in magazines all over the world. A former elementary-school teacher, Christin has written more than twenty-five books for children on a wide range of topics, including sports, science, and history. She makes her home in Sarasota, Florida.

Photographs © 2003: American Heritage Center, University of Wyoming: 39; AP/Wide World Photos/Mark Duncan: 6 bottom; Bridgeman Art Library International Ltd., London/New York: 37 Private Collection), 35 (Royal Geographical Society, London, UK), 15, 28 (The Stapleton Collection); Corbis Images/Scott T. Smith: 13 top; Denver Public Library, Western History Collection in partnership with the Colorado Historical Society, and the Denver Art Museum: 19 right, 19 left; Hulton|Archive/Getty Images: 36 bottom; Nativestock.com/Marilyn "Angel" Wynn: cover, 1, 2, 6 top, 11, 12, 17 top, 17 bottom, 21, 22 bottom, 22 top right, 22 top left, 25, 27, 29, 33, 36 top, 41, 43 top, 43 bottom; Nevada Historical Society: 30; North Wind Picture Archives: 13 bottom; Smithsonian Institution, Washington, DC: 9 bottom (National Anthropological Archives, #1668, photo by W.H. Jackson); Superstock, Inc.: 9 top.
Map by Bob Italiano.